Shy Sam the Wolfdog

By

Alexa Rayburn

Illustrated by Clara Kay

Photography by Alexander Kay

Edited by Louise D. Stahl

COPYRIGHT 2022 BY ALEXA RAYBURN

ALL RIGHTS RESERVED. No part of this publication may be reproduced, distributed, or transmitted in any form or by any means, including photocopying, recording, or other electronic or mechanical methods without the prior written permission of the publisher, except in the case of brief quotations embodied in critical reviews and certain non-commercial uses permitted by copyright law. For permission requests, write to the publisher. Address the request to: "Attention: Permissions Coordinator" at the address below.

Ingram
1 Ingram Boulevard
LaVerge, Tennessee 37086

www.ingramcontent.com

Publisher's Note: This is a work of fiction. Names, characters, places, and incidents are a product of the author's imagination. Location and public names are sometimes used for atmospheric purpose. Any resemblance to any person living or dead is coincidental.

Thanks to Peter and Joan

for sharing this story of

devotion, loyalty, and bravery.

"Do not go where the path might lead, go instead where there is no path and leave a trail."

–Ralph Waldo Emerson

Listen! Listen, my child, to the winds blowing softly across Tampa Bay. They swirl over the Weeki Wachee River, these winds, and are cooled by turquoise springs flowing from deep within the earth. The waters of the Weeki Wachee are dotted with gray manatees feasting on native vegetation. The shores of the river are decorated with feathery, light-green cypress and waxy sweetbay trees.

Listen! Listen, my child, as the winds blow softly, bringing the tale of a wolfdog, timid and shy. This lonely, sad wolfdog had no purpose, no family, no friends. He had no hope, this shy wolfdog named **Sam**.

The warm winds of western Florida *howl* his story across the waters of the Weeki Wachee River. Named by the Seminole Native Americans, the Muskogee word "Wekiwa" means spring and "chee" means little. Legends from long ago tell of mermaids and manatees in these crystal waters, the deepest springs in all the western hemisphere.

The origins of the warm springs of the Weeki Wachee have yet to be discovered. It is here our story begins, where the mysterious waters leap from unseen depths of the earth and rise between the cool winds of spring and the blistering heat waves of summer. Somewhere, between the manatees, the mermaids, and the warm winds begins our story of Shy Sam the wolfdog. Not a dog for a family, not a wolf for the wild with a pack of his own, but an in-between outcast, with no place to belong.

Wolfdog Sam was born to a gray wolf mother who found herself with not one, but *three* pups. The first pup, Willow, was a rough and tumble fighter. The second, Sierra, was a loner who couldn't be bothered with a needy brother. And Sam? Little Sam couldn't fight for his place. It wasn't his nature; he couldn't and he *wouldn't*.

The kind woman who loved the pups wished she could keep them, but *three* pups were too much for her small house. With a sad heart, she called for strangers who could help her. The strangers had special knowledge to help her take care of newborn wolfdog pups.

The crying, weeping winds moaned sadly as they swirled through the night from the Weeki Wachee. Tears and heavy rain fell as the wolfdog pups were taken from their mother. With one sad, long look, they said goodbye. The kind strangers took the young wolfdog pups to the Gray Wolf Rescue; a place where unwanted animals could be given comfort and care, feeding and love.

Deep in the heart of southwest Florida at The Gray Wolf Rescue, the wolfdog pups were sheltered and safe. The winds from the Weeki Wachee blew strong, but calm. Despite the comfort carried on the winds, Sam and his sisters continued to fight. His larger and stronger sisters could and *would* take all of his food. Sadly, the shy wolf with no family, no pack, and no hope, grew quite tired.

Little Shy Sam curled into a spiky ball of fur,
and just gave up.

The summer winds blew mean and angry, and thunder rumbled along the coast. But then, quietly, one rainy Florida night, a man and his wife came to see Shy Sam. It was the woman, Joan, who went into the pen first. She sat very still, taking her time and speaking softly. Serene and quiet, she sat in the pen for what seemed like *forever*. She reached out her hand, but he was timid and *so* scared. Her voice brought comfort through the mist on the rainy summer night.

The young wolfdog finally moved toward her hand. Then, her husband Peter came quietly into the pen and held out his hand. Sam, little Sam, shook and trembled with fear. He quivered as they lifted him and wrapped him in a soft, warm blanket. They spoke so softly that he closed his eyes, not wanting to face the strangers. For the first time, he felt a *little* bit safe as the Weeki Wachee winds ruffled his fur protectively.

So it was Joan who spoke first, in a whisper. "Yes, we can take him. It's got to be now, before it's too late. There is no other choice, he's too frightened to eat."

Peter agreed. They would take the wolfdog home, they would give him a chance. The winds of the Weeki Wachee swirled around Sam softly and kindly, telling the pup not to be afraid. He was placed on a soft blanket in a carrier. Even so, the terrified little wolfdog cowered and shook with fear while Joan and Peter quickly drove home.

The car stopped in the driveway. Gentle hands reached in for him and lifted him out. Too frightened to open his eyes, he felt them set him on the ground. Terrified, he could barely stand. He opened his eyes and peeked out. Walking a few steps, he stretched his legs. Peter remained beside him and Joan brought him water and a small dish of food. But, Sam was too frightened to eat. The soft, gentle winds ruffled his fur, and he felt a little reassured.

"Come inside," said Peter, but Sam froze. He couldn't move his legs. Peter gently lifted him up and carried him inside, while Joan followed behind.

They placed him safely on the same soft blanket in a larger crate in the living room. Food and water were placed close to him, while Peter and Joan sat on the floor nearby to watch.

"You know, he needs quiet and comfort," Peter said softly.

"You are safe now, Sam," said Joan as she smiled at him, "and this can be your home." She stretched her fingers through the bars to let him smell them as she repeated the words, "*this can be your home!*"

In the other room, two sets of eyes were glowing and frozen. The eyes seemed to be watching him. But what were they? Sam trembled with fear, but sensed they were friendly eyes and he relaxed just a bit. He was afraid to stand and walk to the water bowl only a few inches away from him, even though he was thirsty. Leaning, scooting, he stretched his neck out as far as he could and lapped at the bowl. He did not make a sound. **But, he felt four piercing eyes staring straight through his heart!**

From their room, Joan and Peter were watching as he lapped his water. They smiled and Joan nodded her head in relief. But still, two pairs of silent, glistening eyes watched. Sam heard the whisper of the soft winds from the springs and they comforted him. "You are safe now wolf, you are safe." He felt the gentle breeze ruffle his fur. He took a deep breath, curled up on his blanket, and went to sleep.

In the morning, it was Shy Sam who woke first. He pulled himself up to stand and carefully, silently, made his way to the water bowl. He saw a gate across the entrance to another room where two large, fluffy dogs were sitting side by side staring at him. *Oh, so those had been the spooky eyes staring in the dark.*

Quickly, he dropped back down, hoping that they hadn't seen him. He tried to sink into his plush blanket to disappear. Suddenly, from yet another doorway, the man walked quietly up to his crate.

"Sam, meet the Germans! Germans, meet Sam! Now, let's all be very quiet so Joan can sleep a bit longer. I'll make the coffee, and we'll get treats." Peter opened the sliding door and two long-haired German Shepherds bounded outside, ignoring the newcomer. Deanna and Timo played in the fenced yard, leaping through the native plants and sniffing the clean sniffs of the morning mist.

"You see Sam, that's how it's done. I open the door, and you go outside! Easy enough, right?"

Sam cowered with fear. The man was bad enough, but the Germans were really something to worry about. Sam cried pitifully. He needed to wet and he didn't want to wet in the crate where he slept.

"What's wrong, Sam?" Peter asked gently. "Are you afraid to leave the crate? Come on now, nothing to fear, the Germans are back inside and they can't get you!"

So, for that morning, and every three hours for many days, Peter carried the small, shy wolfdog outside, where Sam could walk a few steps and relieve himself. Whimpering softly when he was finished, Sam could not bring himself to walk back to the house. He listened for the winds to blow softly from the Weeki Wachee Springs, but the winds were silent. Who would guide him? As he looked up, there was Peter, waiting to carry Shy Sam.

The Germans, Deanna and Timo, eyed Sam suspiciously. They listened for the smallest sound the wolfpup would make. They heard him whimpering and crying when the loneliness came, even though Peter and Joan spent hours talking to him. Joan would read him stories and pet his head. The swirling winds from the Weeki Wachee Springs skimmed over the waters of the river and found their way to Sam. They reminded him that somewhere out there, wolves were living in packs, and part of him would *always* be a wolf.

Timo and Deanna pondered the situation, and had a serious discussion about the fate of the wolfdog pup. They agreed on a plan. They would try to come closer to Sam and allow him to use his dog senses to see they weren't a threat. *We have enough love in this house to share. We're not gonna let that pup struggle!* The next time Sam was in the yard they would beg to be let out too, and they would slowly approach him! Lightning, the house cat, listened from the windowsill. It was her business to keep an eye on all of them.

But in the morning, before they had a chance to carry out their plan, Peter and Joan put Shy Sam into his carrier. As Timo and Deanna watched from the window, they saw Sam loaded into the car. Joan and Peter quickly drove away. *We've lost our chance!* They looked at each other sadly. *No more little pup!* They both dropped to the floor and bayed loudly. Even Lightning was missing the little pup and she covered her face with her paws.

What the Germans did not, and could not, know was that Shy Sam had been taken to the veterinarian for his check-up. He was weighed, examined, poked and prodded, and given shots to keep him from becoming sick. He was pronounced in great health. The doctor spoke with Peter and Joan about the foods he was to eat, and how to introduce him gradually to Timo and Deanna. Sam was slowly but surely becoming part of the family.

But then, through the fall, the winter winds of the Weeki Wachee called Sam again. The soft winds blew quietly in his ear and ruffled his fur. They reminded him that part of him belonged to the wild, the part of him that would *always* remain a wolf. Deanna and Timo watched nervously as their friend, now their brother, listened to the call. Being Shepherd dogs, they heard the whispers of the wild too, and they felt the soft ruffling of their fur. They ignored it and turned toward their masters. As dogs have done for centuries, they vowed to lay down their lives for Peter and Joan.

Soon, Peter was the one to do the teaching. The winds of the wild told Sam that finding food was not to be taken for granted. Peter taught Sam that food would be forthcoming daily, and he could rely on a meal. As Deanna and Timo watched, Peter made Sam wait his turn as he fed each dog. Sam learned that he could trust Peter to feed him, and trust Timo and Deanna not to take his food. He learned he would not have to survive on his own.

Deanna and Timo learned to dig under the bridge in the backyard as Sam taught them to dig a hidey-hole. A wolf needs a warm place to sleep when the coldness comes. Sam taught Deanna and Timo skills that wolves need to survive.

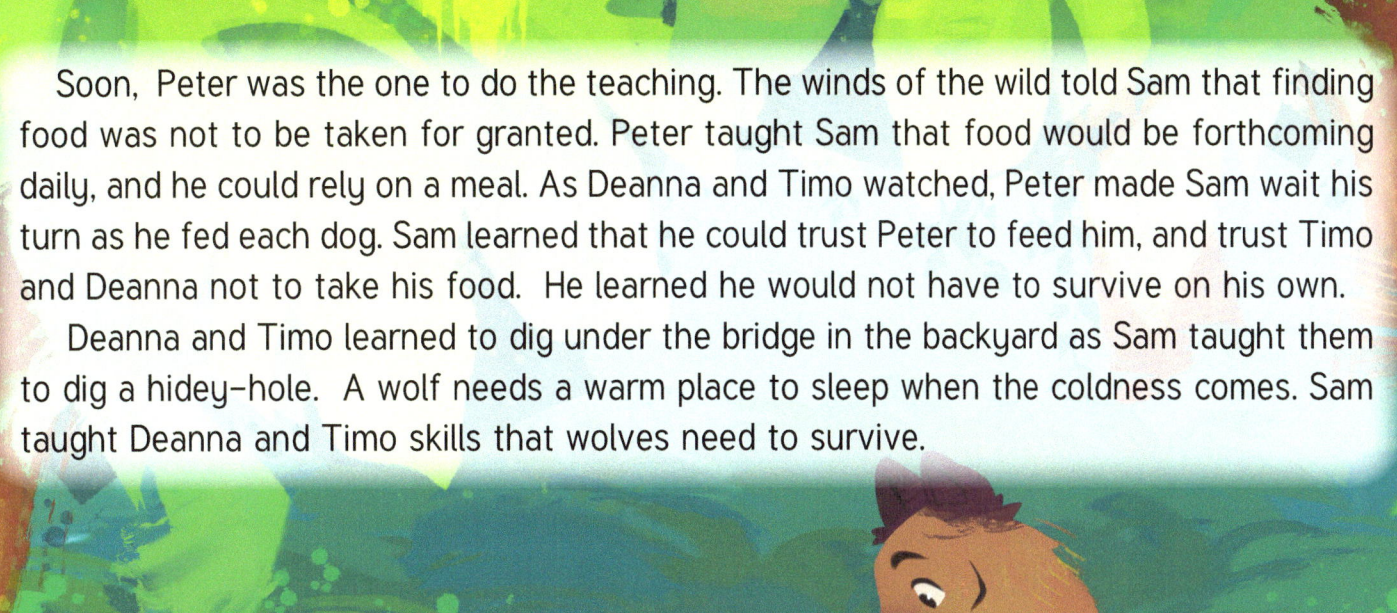

In the winter, as Timo, Deanna, Joan, and Peter tutored Sam, he grew taller, stronger, and more agile. He could run faster and jump higher than the Germans. His long, lanky legs could spring him up from the ground. They watched with approval as their pupil grew into a strong, handsome dog, a loyal dog who respected his humans. Shy Sam the wolfdog learned to trust and love the humans who gave him their hearts. The two Germans, as well as Lightning the cat, all joined Peter and Joan to become Sam's pack.

As the winter gave way to spring, the winds of the Weeki Wachee Springs called to Shy Sam again. They called to the part of him that he could never deny: the wolf. The dog, they mercifully let be. As the warm winds of spring called to him, he paced more, he searched more, and he was restless.

The winds breathed softly, speaking in a voice that only Sam could hear. *You are one with the wind, wolf. You have a place in the wild, and every wolf belongs in a pack. Listen to us, Sam the wolfdog. Listen! Listen!!!*

It was at times like this when Peter and Joan would smile as Sam would plant his two front feet, raise his nose to the air, and howl the wind a reply.

Awooo... Awooo... Awooo... he would answer, as Lightning the cat covered his ears with his paws and waited for him to stop.

Shy Sam took a strong liking to the firetruck that screamed as it raced through the community. At first, he listened intently to the high-pitched squeal of the siren. But eventually, he placed his front paws firmly in front of him, raised his nose high into the sky, and answered back their screams. Timo, Deanna, Joan, Peter, and Lightning all watched in amazement as Sam mimicked the siren and answered the call.

It was while playing ball with Peter, or running in the yard with Timo and Deanna, or lounging by the pool with Lightning, that Shy Sam the wolfdog made peace with the gentle, soft winds. No matter if he was resting quietly in the living room with Joan, or following Timo and Deanna in the yard, the soft winds of the Weeki Wachee found him and whispered their songs in his ear. One day, as the others watched, he raised his nose to the air and answered them back.

I have found my home, gentle winds, and I have found my pack. It matters not who is pack leader. Maybe it is Peter, perhaps it is Timo, or maybe it is my gentle Joan. But, my pack watches over me as I sleep peacefully, protected by their love. Gentle arms surround me in a circle of care. You can call me anytime, winds, and I will listen, for you are my heritage. But I am safe and happy here with those who protect me with their lives. And I, Shy Sam the wolfdog, will give my life and my honor to them in return.

Shy Sam the wolfdog had found his pack. He had found his home. He was here to stay.

Children's Page

When we talk about a wolfdog, we are talking about an animal that is part dog and part wolf. If we have an animal that is 75% wolf and 25% dog, we expect that animal to act more like a wolf than a dog. If we have an animal that is 75% dog and 25% wolf, we expect it to act more like a dog. Sometimes, it may not be clear what percentage of the animal is wolf or dog, and predicting their behavior is impossible.

Dogs have developed a close relationship with man. They are companions and protectors, and become very close to their human families. This may not be true with an animal that has a higher percentage of wolf. In the wild, wolves fear man and they are less likely to live peacefully with humans.

It may seem like a novel idea to have a wolfdog as a pet. However, this is a pet for a person experienced with raising both wolves *and* dogs. A wolfdog is a pet that requires a great deal of knowledge. The feeding requirements and space requirements of a wolf are very different from a dog and can be both expensive and time-consuming.

The best way to understand these animals is to volunteer at local animal shelters. Understanding dogs is a good first step. As you become experienced with the behavior of dogs, it may be possible to visit a wolf sanctuary and observe these magnificent animals. It may be possible to train like Joan did, and work with wolves. These animals need our protection and are best served if we understand the unique needs of these magnificent hybrid animals.

All About Wolfdogs

Magnificent exceptionalism. When listening to the story of Shy Sam the incredible wolfdog, one is struck by his exceptionalism, as well as the exceptionalism of Peter and Joan. This is no ordinary wolfdog, and these are extraordinary people. Unforgettable is the devotion that the couple and their dogs share. Unforgettable as well are the over 300,000 wolfdogs who don't share such a remarkable fate.

Sam was fortunate in that he crossed paths with Joan, a dedicated volunteer who had served tirelessly at an animal sanctuary. She had earned her way up through the ranks of the trainers able to handle wolves. She learned to assess their needs and unpredictability. Peter, her husband, let her take the lead as they brought Sam into the family structure.

The integration of Sam into Peter and Joan's life was literally perfect. There were no small children in the home. The animals who already lived there, two irascible German Shepherds, were already devoted to Peter and Joan. As the story goes, they showed Sam about being a dog and Shy Sam showed the Germans the wolf side of himself. He taught them skills a wolf needs to survive.

Currently in the United States, there are more than fifty sanctuaries that accept wolfdogs. There are 250,000 to 500,000 wolfdogs living as pets. Why do many wolfdogs find their way to either euthanization, or in the alternative, sanctuary? Quite simply, the requirements of the animal outweigh what the inexperienced owner is able to provide. Ninety percent of wolfdogs are euthanized by the age of two, when the romanticized idea of sharing a home with these magnificent creatures requires more than was expected.

While the thrill of wolfdog ownership is exhilarating, eventually the requirements of the breed can become insurmountable. The animal that was supposed to become a member of the family is shunned, caged, or euthanized. Lucky wolfdogs are accepted into sanctuary. They roam free and are pampered by willing volunteers.

What is the evolutionary and breeding history of the wolfdog that makes keeping one problematic? Wolves and dogs progressed along different evolutionary paths. While wolves developed skills to enable them to survive *without* man, dogs developed skills to survive *with* man. When the two species were interbred at first, it was in the hopes of creating a super animal, and it occurred in four distinct parts of the world.

In the Arctic, Malamutes were interbred with wolves to produce a superior freight dog. A *Wolamute* is a cross between a Malamute and a gray wolf. It is the oldest wolf-hybrid in the world. In Russia, the first *Volkasoby* wolfdog was a product of a special breeding program in the 1990s. The first two hundred offspring retained the wolf trait of fear of humans and the program was pronounced a failure. Then, a Caspian wolf called *Nada* was obtained by scientists and this derivative gray wolf was bred to a German Shepherd. The resultant pups were a success. The wolfdogs were bred to protect the Russian Border, and ownership was limited to soldiers on the front. *Nada* was the mother of no less than forty pups and the pups retained the Shepherd's obedience to man, but exhibited the ferocity of the mother. These pups were interbred down to a specific twenty-five percent wolf.

Similarly, the Czechs in 1955 bred a Carpathian Gray Wolf to a German Shepherd. The intent was to breed a border patrol dog, not to establish a new breed of pet. The initial offspring favored the wolf, but subsequent breeding with more German Shepherds led to a bloodline which was 6.25% wolf. These wolfdogs maintained the loyalty of the Shepherd, but retained the strength, agility, and endurance of

the Carpathian Gray Wolf. They were accepted in 1982 as a new breed, and are still popular.

In the United States, breeding was haphazard; there was no deliberate plan as there was in Russia and Czechoslovakia. Poorly intentioned "breeders" created lines with unknown percentages of wolf. They based the breeding on the physical attractiveness and marketability of the animal, rather than the characteristics desired. Pandemonium ruled, and still rules to this day. Different states have different rules for owning a wolfdog; some ban them entirely. The internet is still a place where animals of unknown lineage are sold for thousands of dollars from wolfdog breeding mills. The unsuspecting buyer may purchase an animal that looks dog-like, but could have a higher amount of wolf behaviors, or alternatively an animal that appears wolf-like, but acts just like any other dog.

The random, careless breeding and sale of these animals has doomed many of them to lives in cages or on chains. Careless, selfish human behavior has created an unfortunate situation for these hybrids. We hope that your appreciation for the wolfdog in this country, 300,000 strong, will grow as we solve the dilemma; a disaster of our own making. There are many reputable wolfdog sanctuaries and conservation programs that would welcome your support. Join them in their mission to protect and nurture these magnificent animals.

www.ingramcontent.com/pod-product-compliance
Lightning Source LLC
Chambersburg PA
CBHW041527070526
44585CB00003B/115